Make Your Disney Career A Reality: How To Draw A Mermaid Book

Draw Mermaids Like a Disney Illustrator: Guide Book

Mermaid Book

By : Gala Publication

Published By :

Gala Publication

© Copyright 2015 – Gala Publication

ISBN-13: **978-1522721536**
ISBN-10: **1522721533**

Table of Contents

4

BABY MERMAID

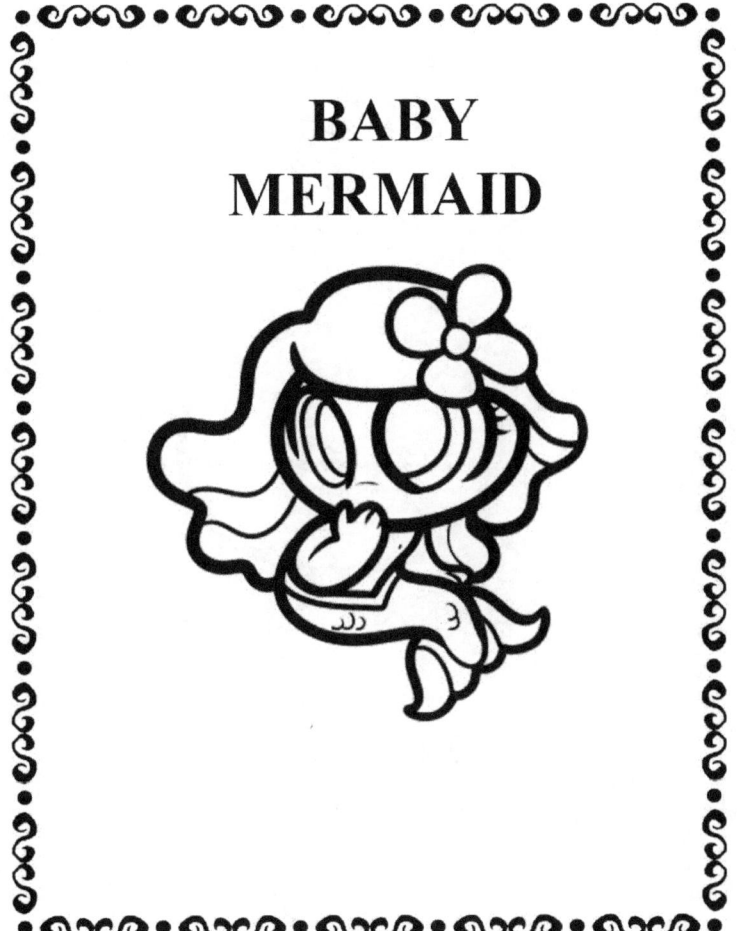

STEP 1

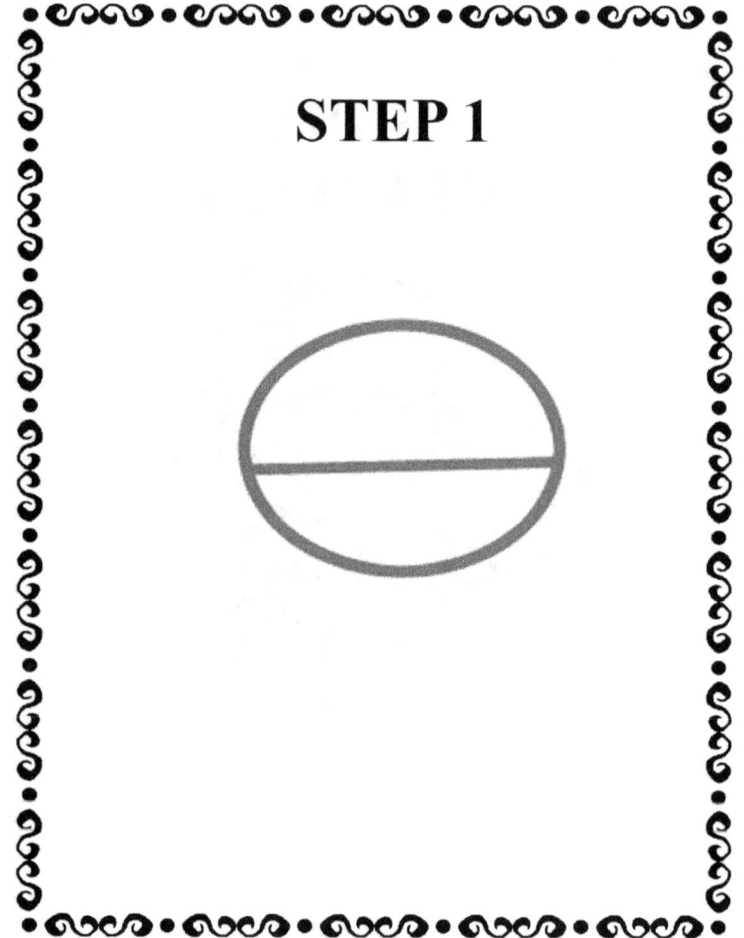

STEP 2

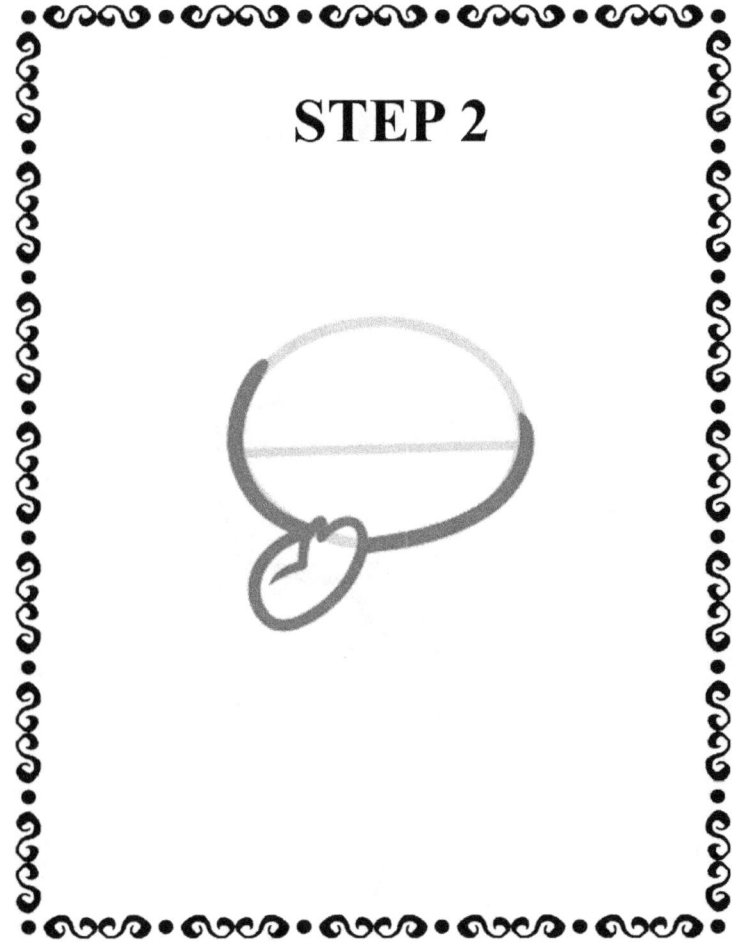

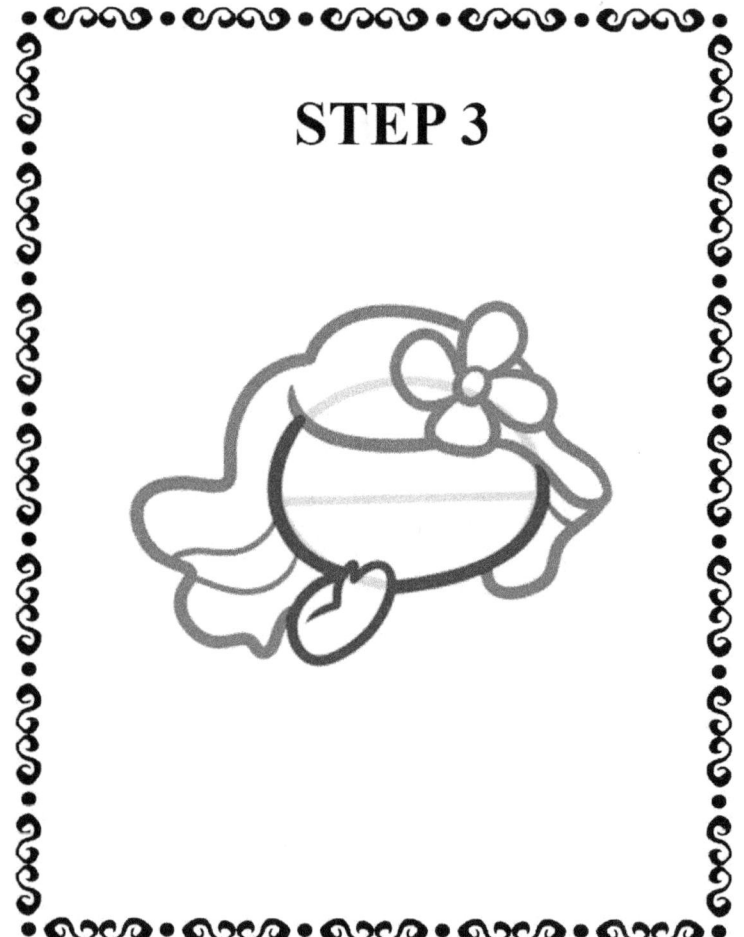

8

STEP 3

STEP 4

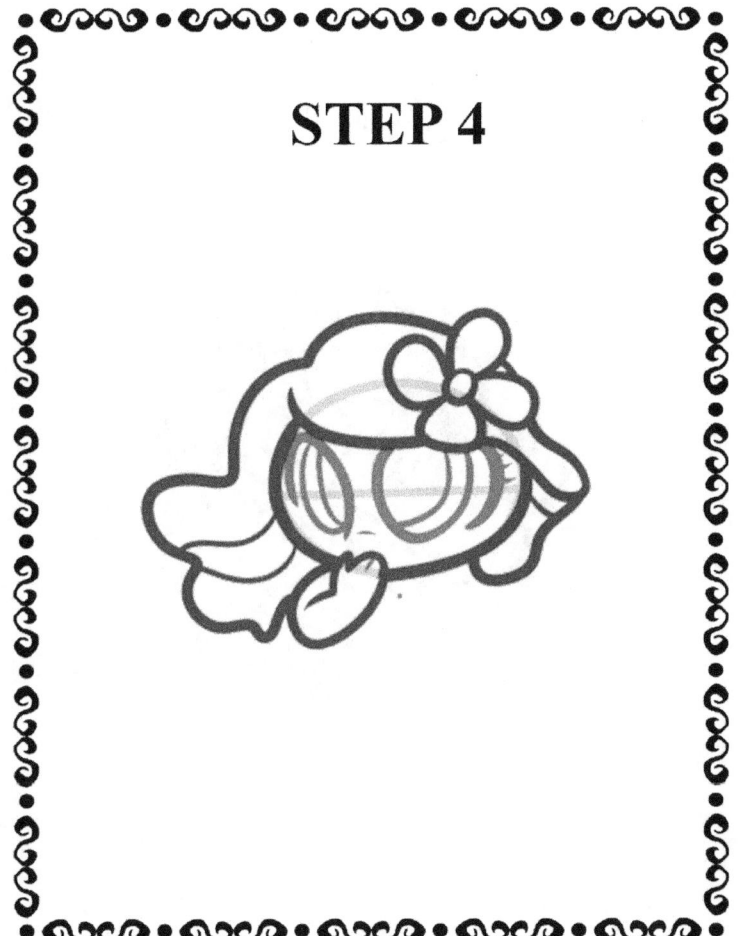

STEP 5

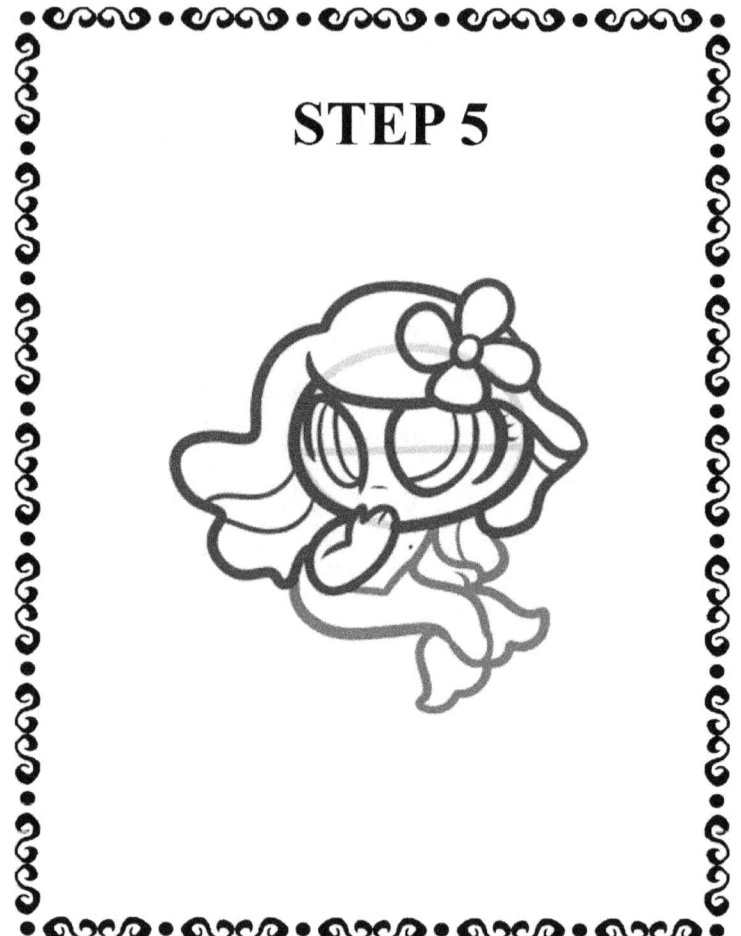

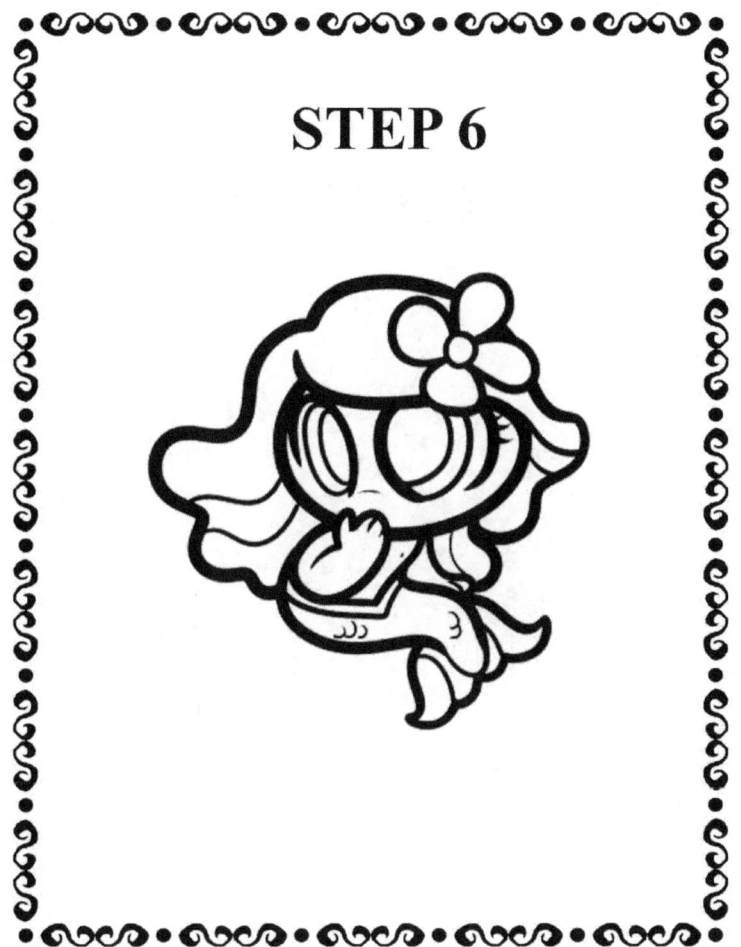

STEP 6

CARTOON
MERMAID

STEP 1

STEP 2

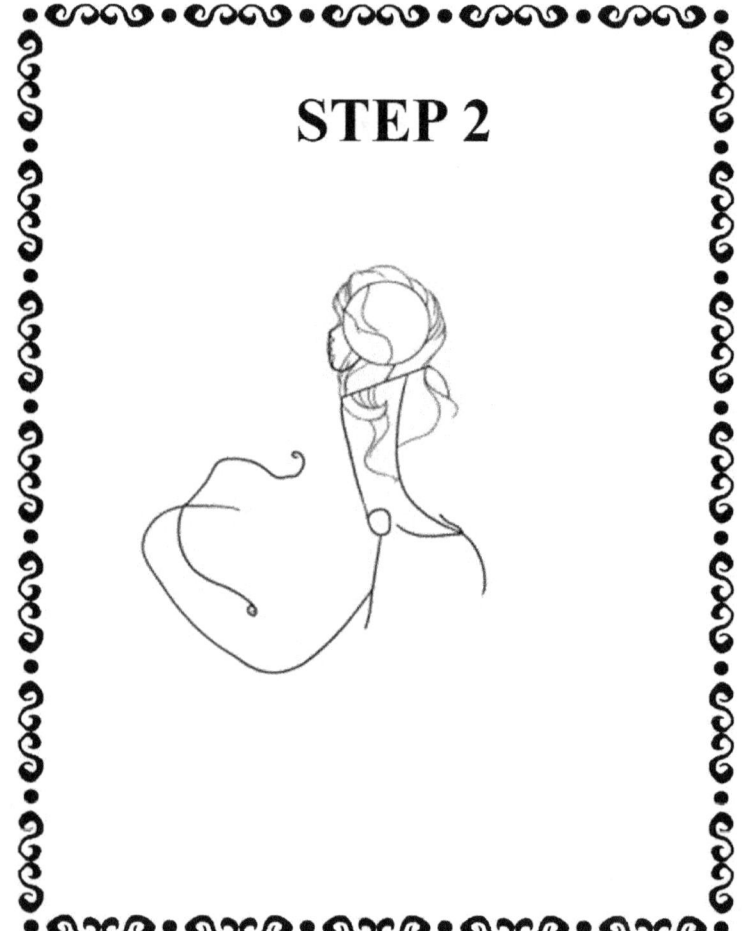

STEP 3

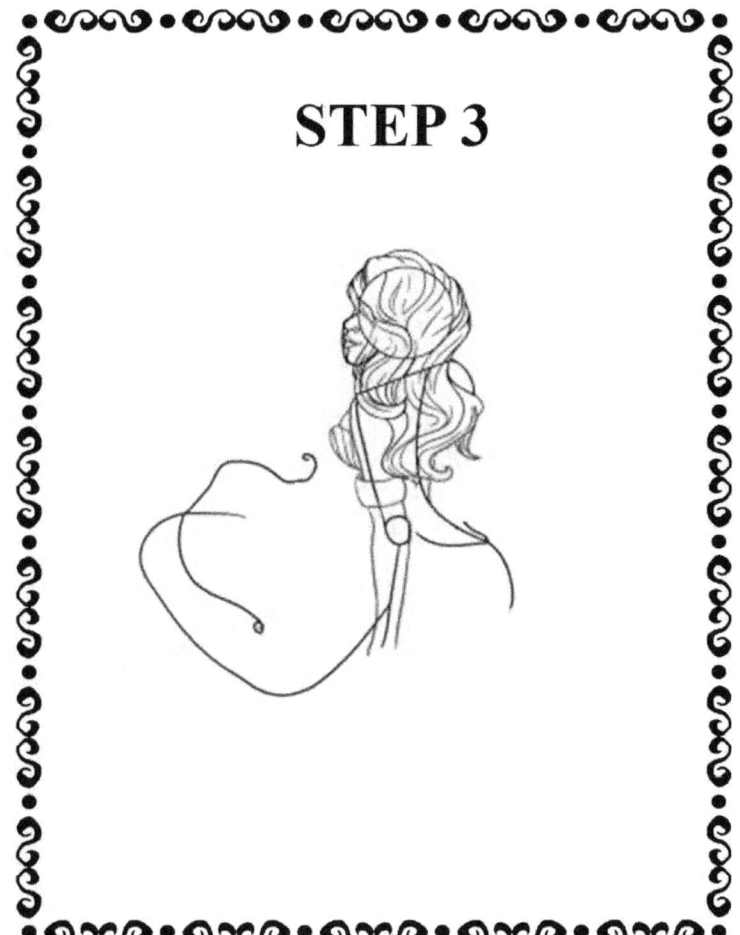

STEP 4

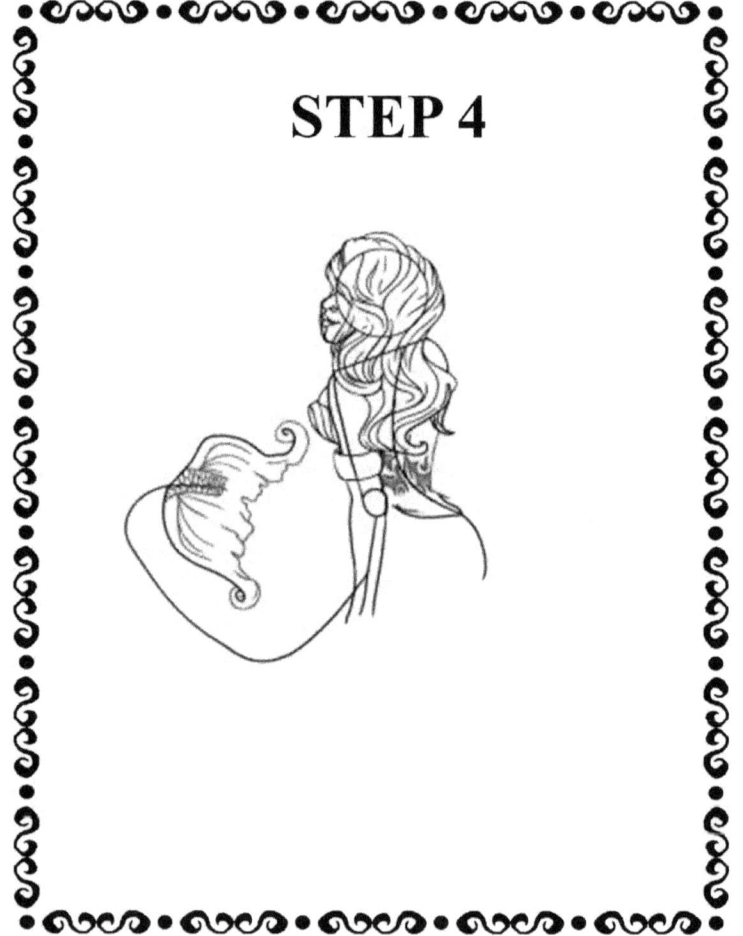

STEP 5

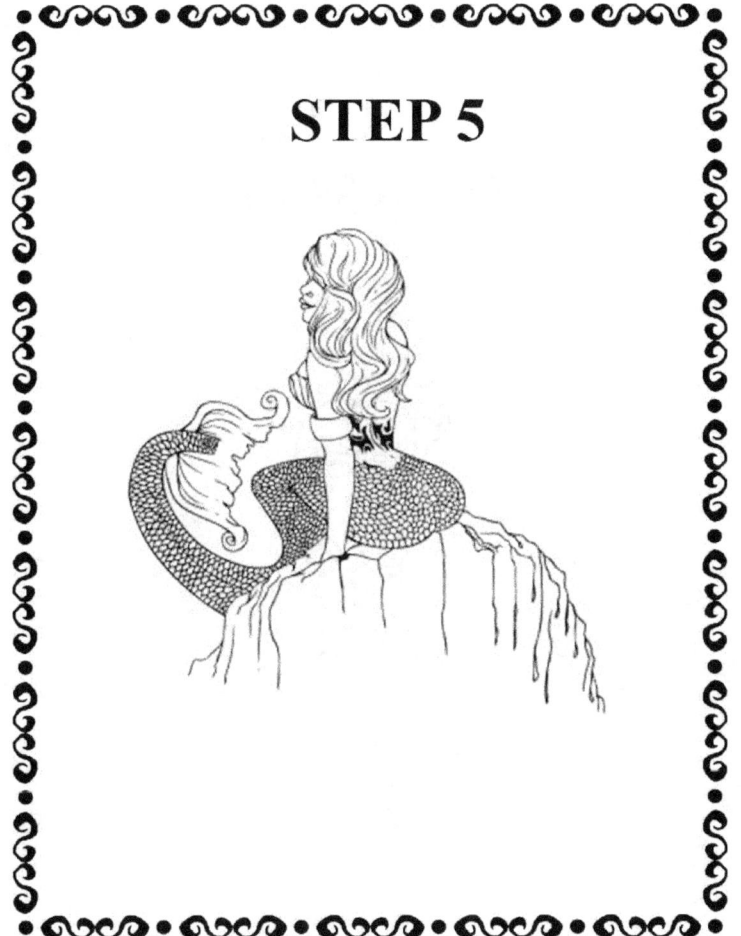

CUTE
MERMAID

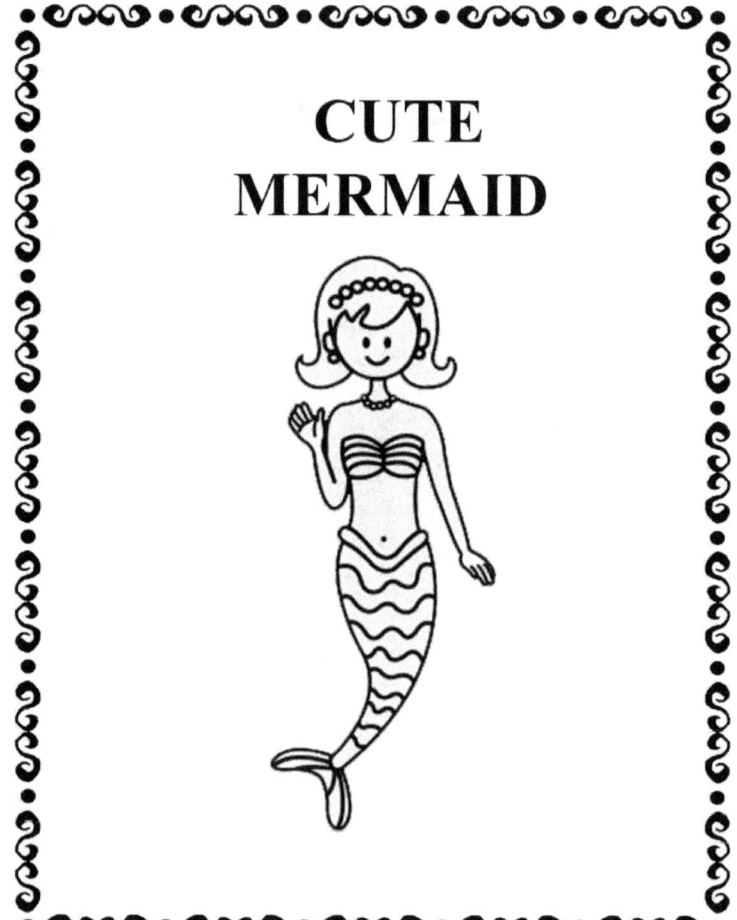

STEP 1

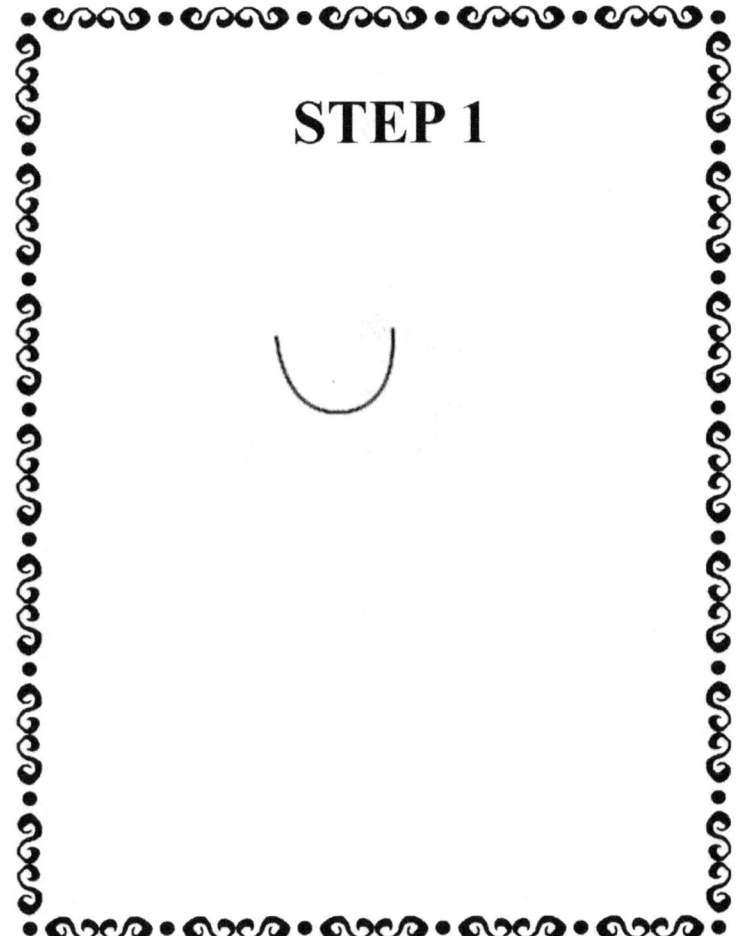

STEP 2

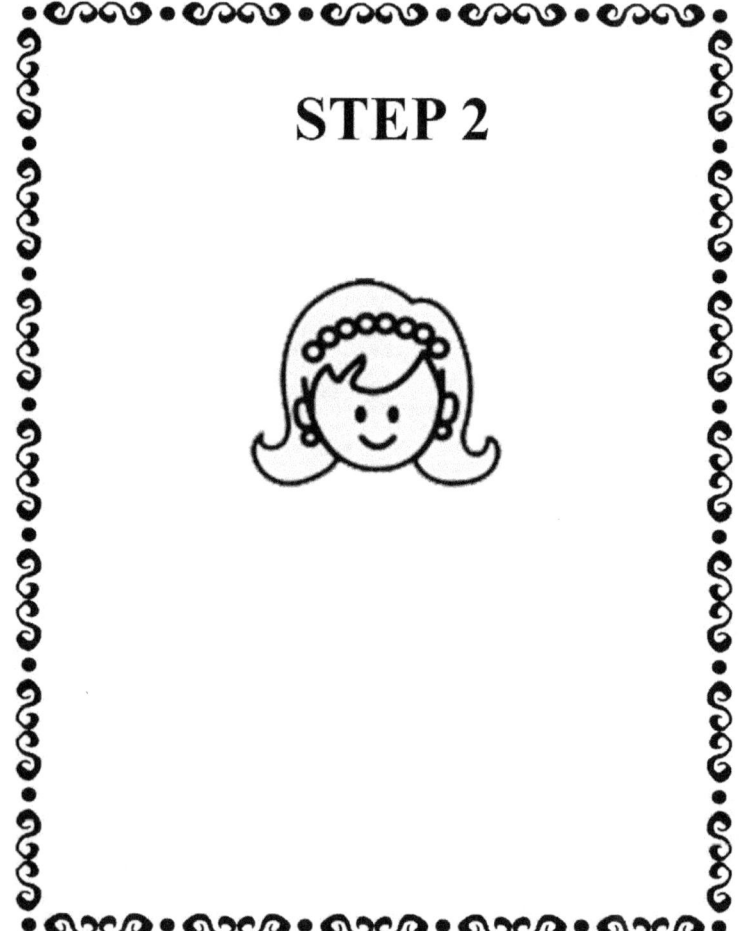

STEP 3

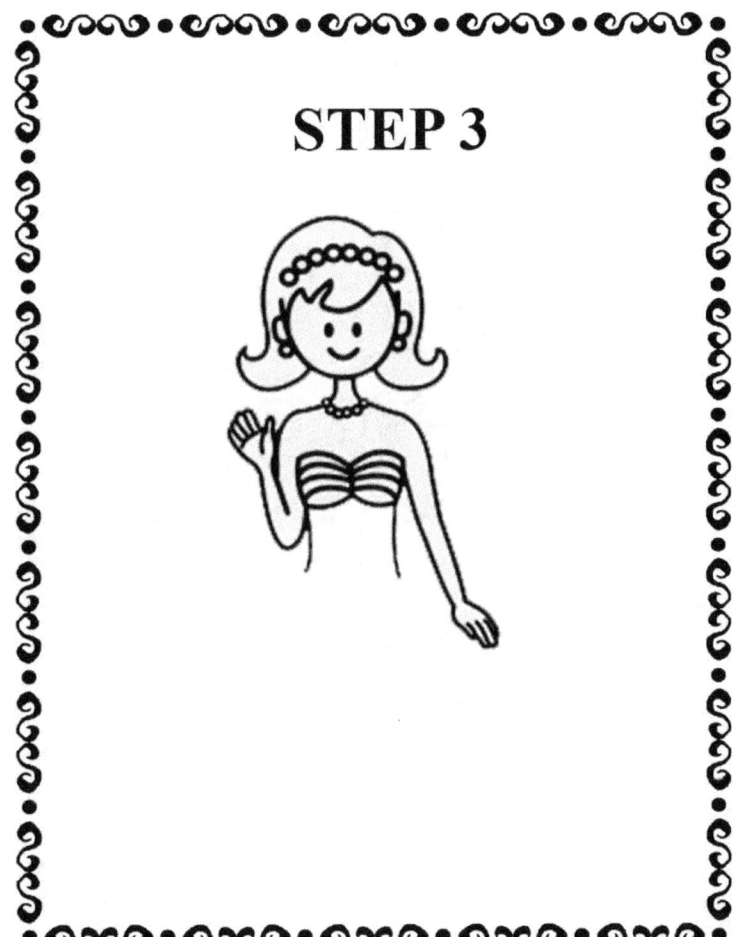

STEP 4

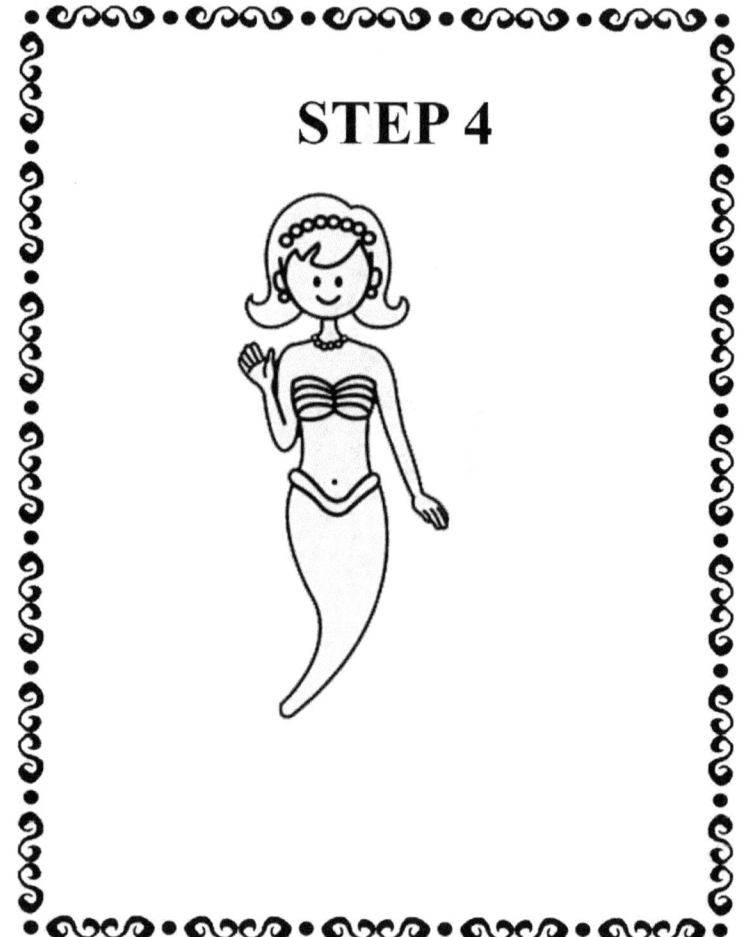

STEP 5

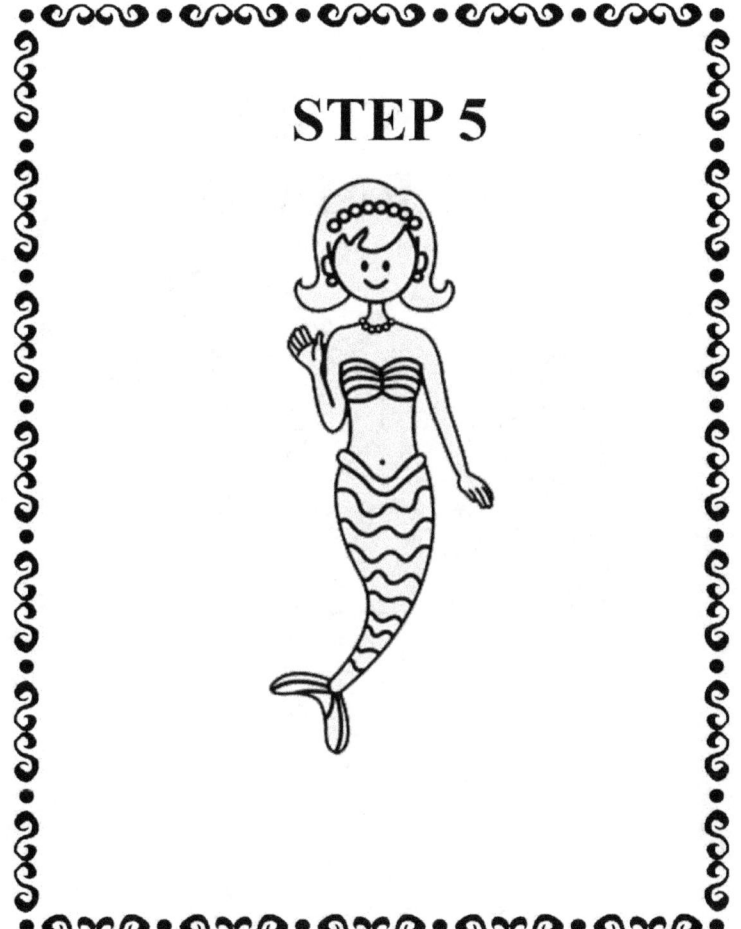

FANTASY MERMAID

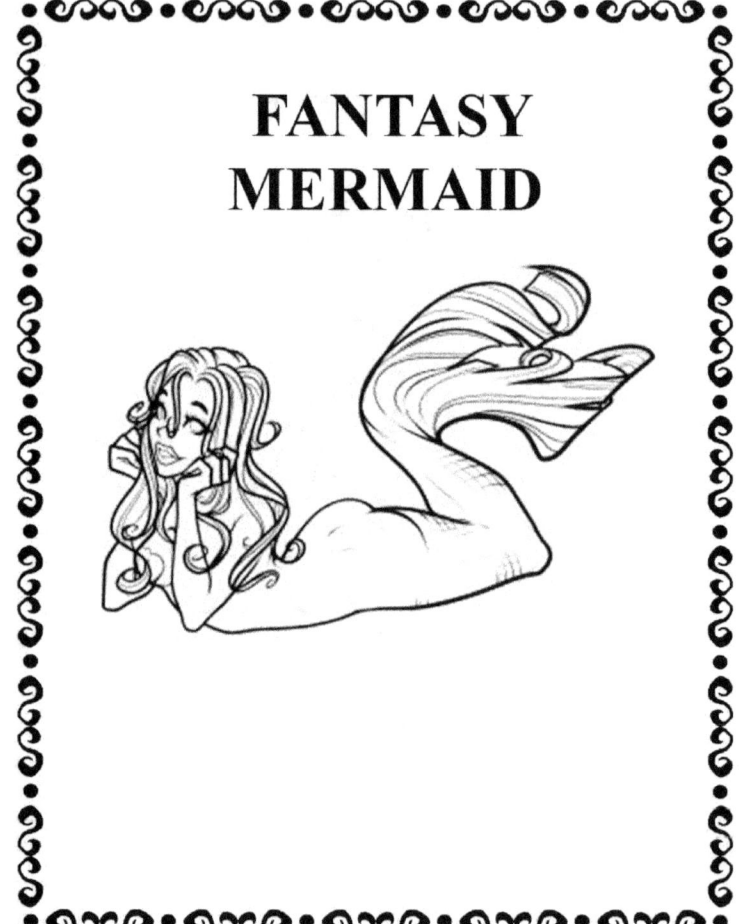

STEP 1

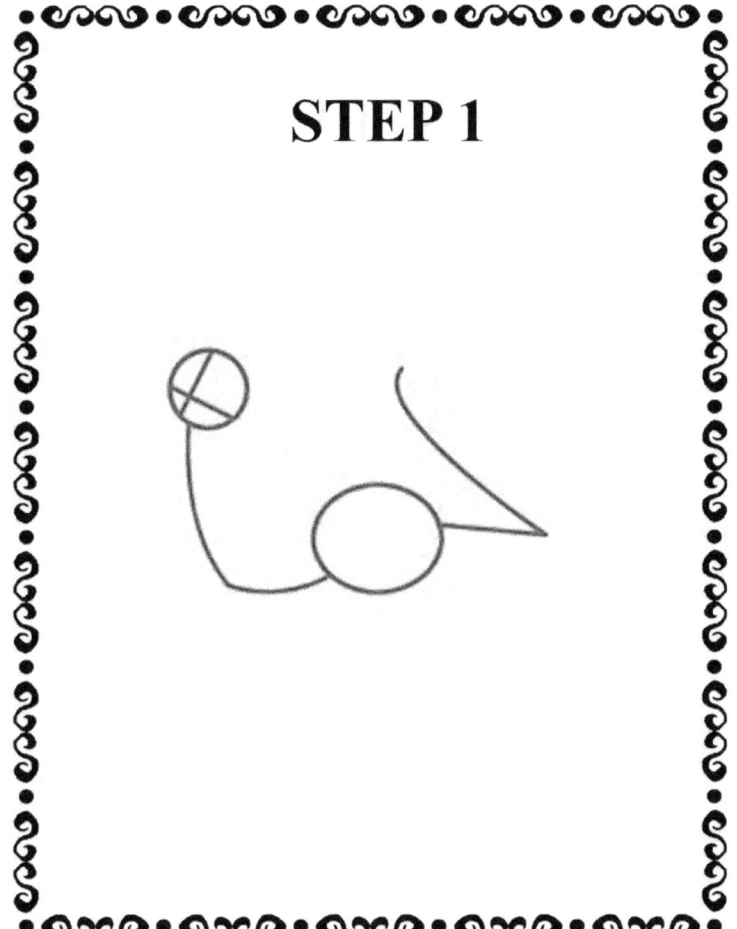

STEP 2

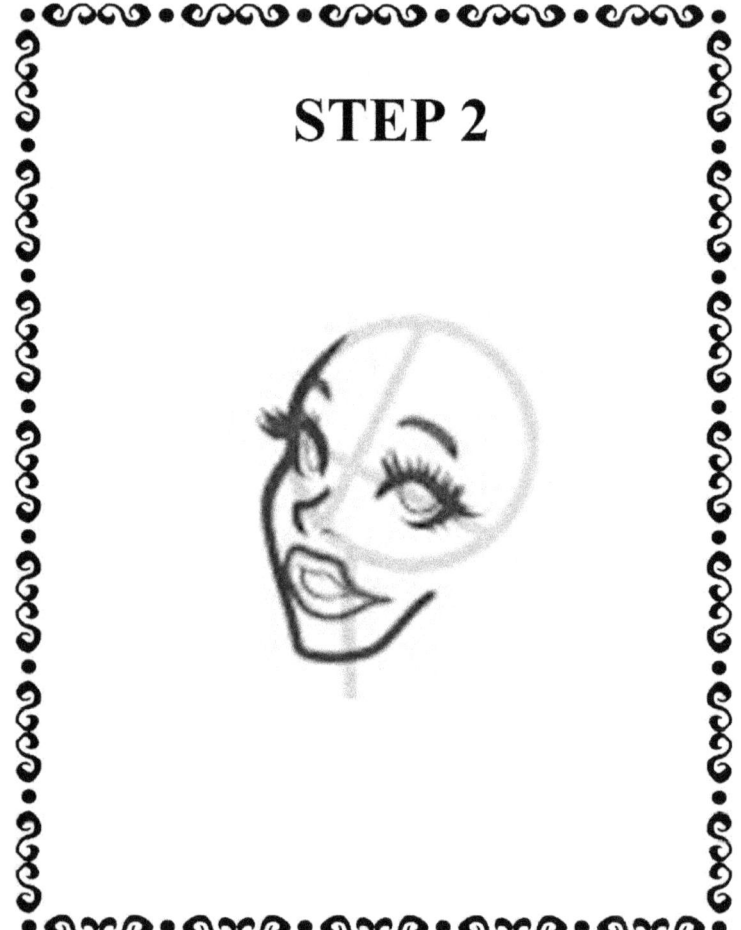

STEP 3

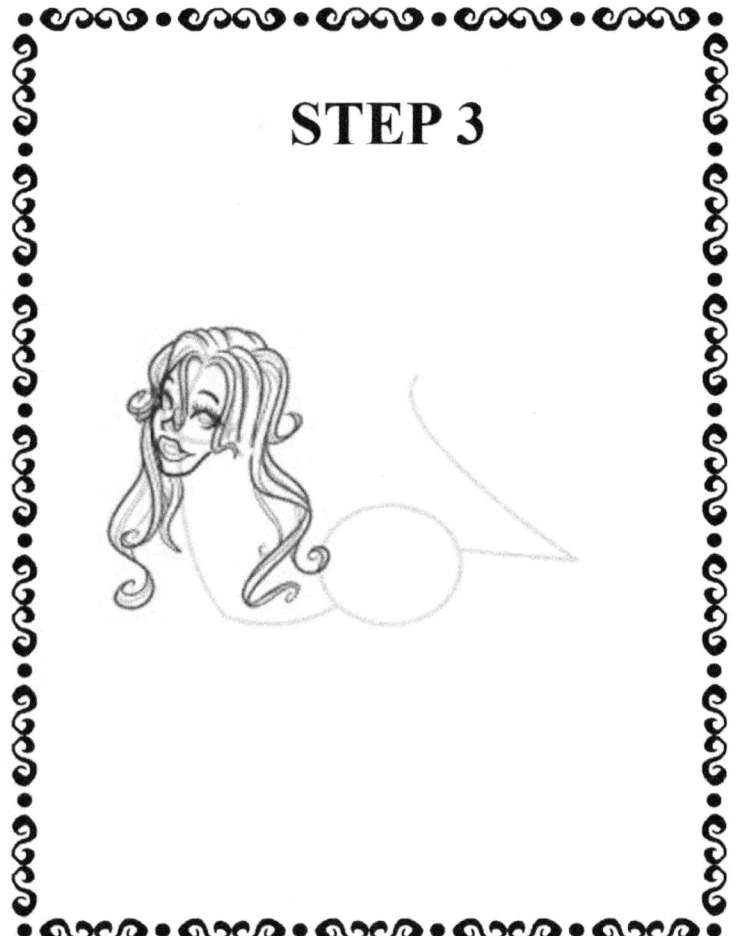

STEP 4

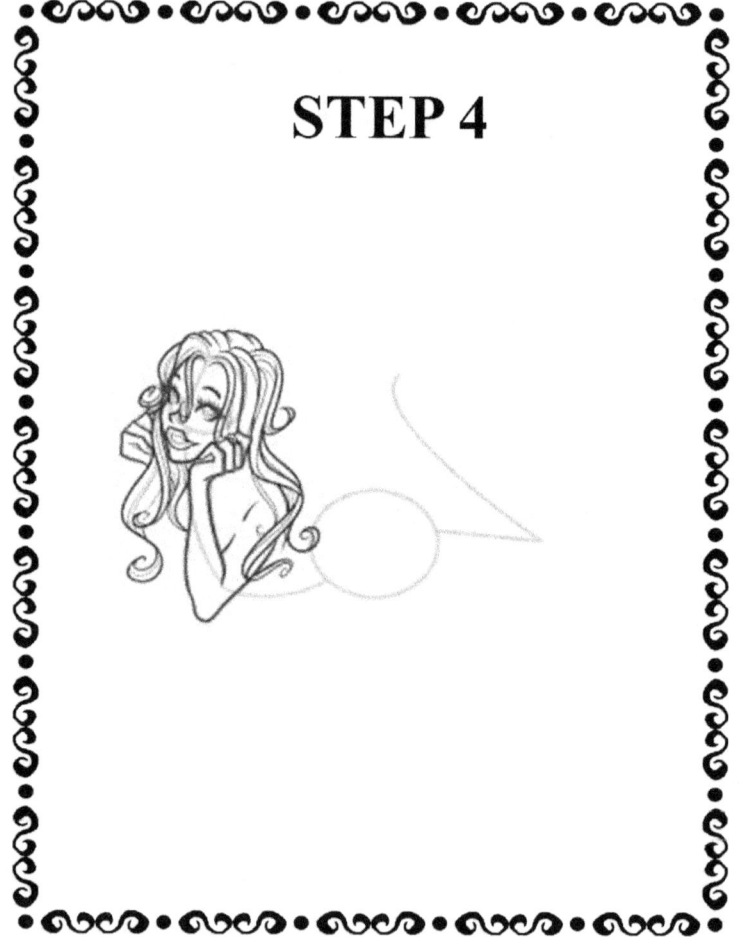

STEP 5

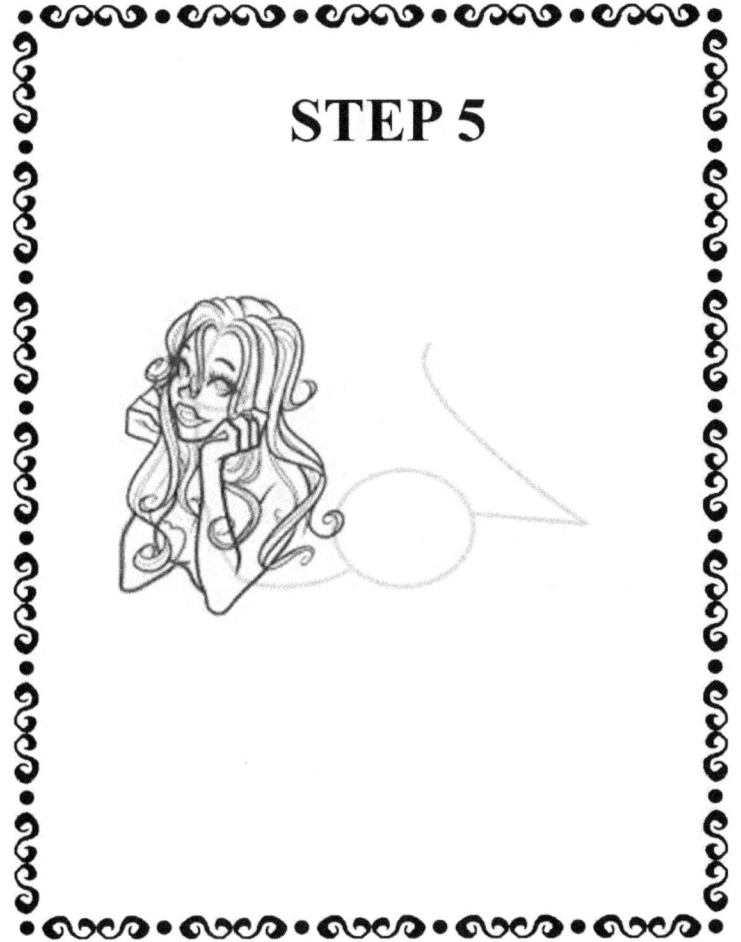

STEP 6

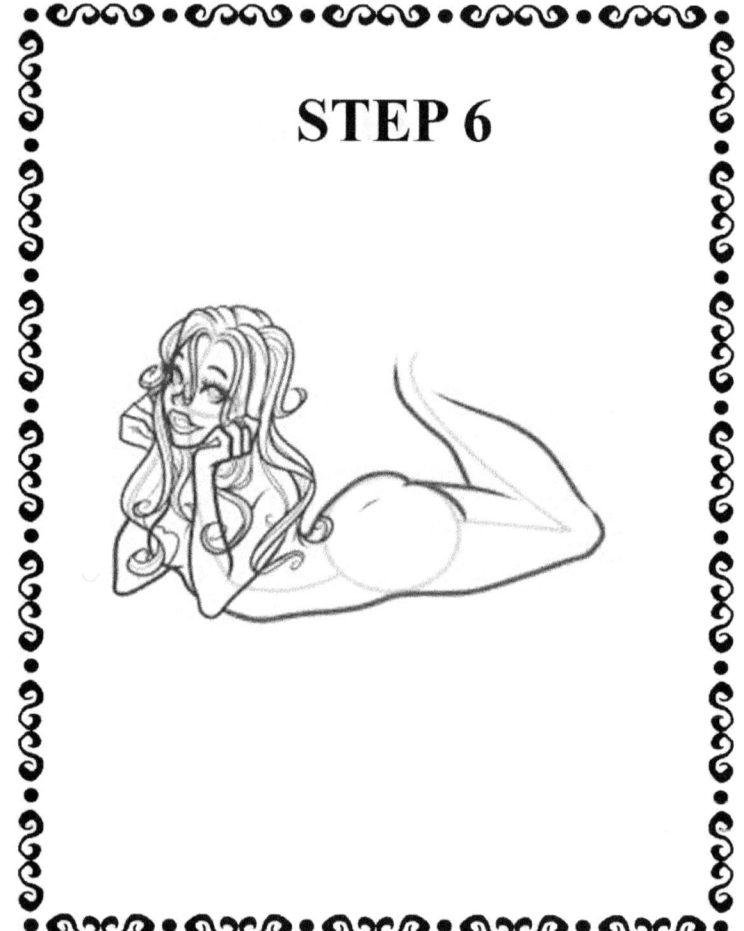

STEP 7

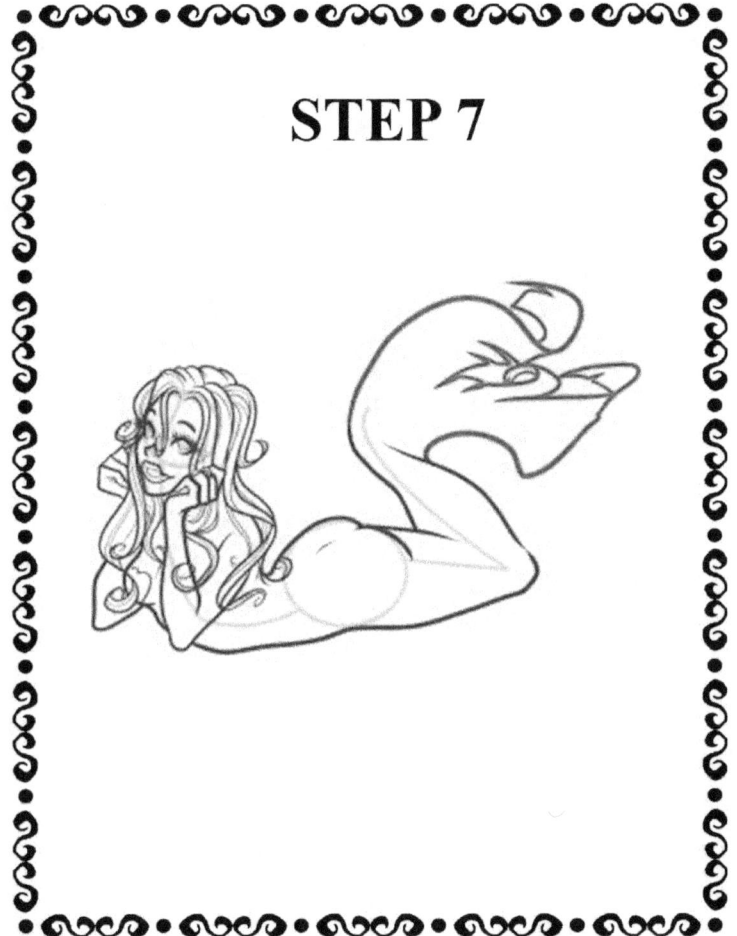

STEP 8

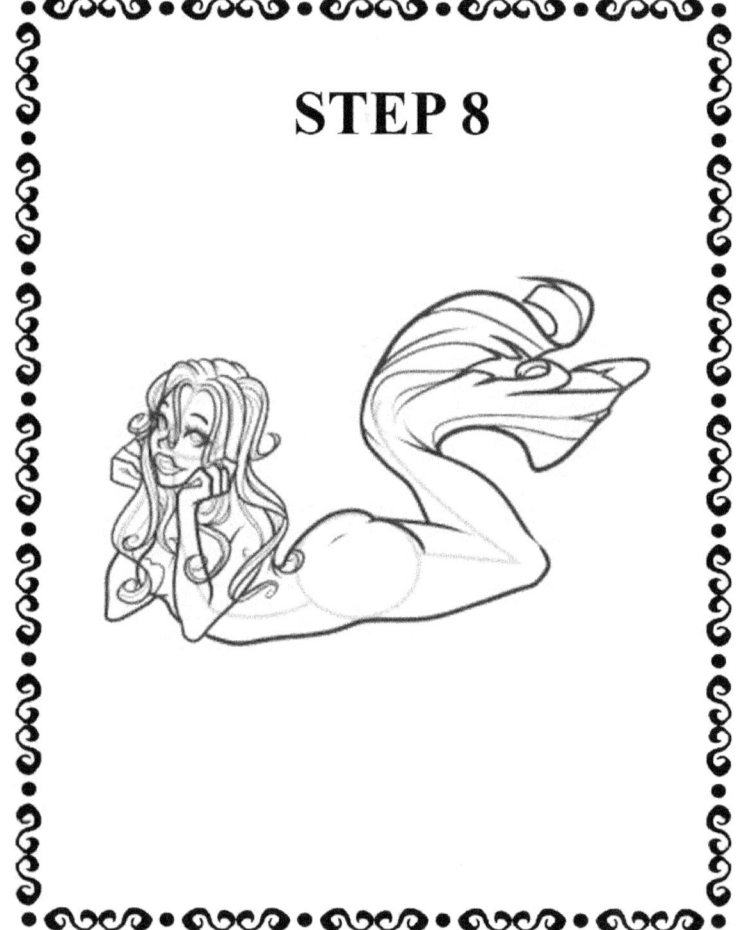

STEP 9

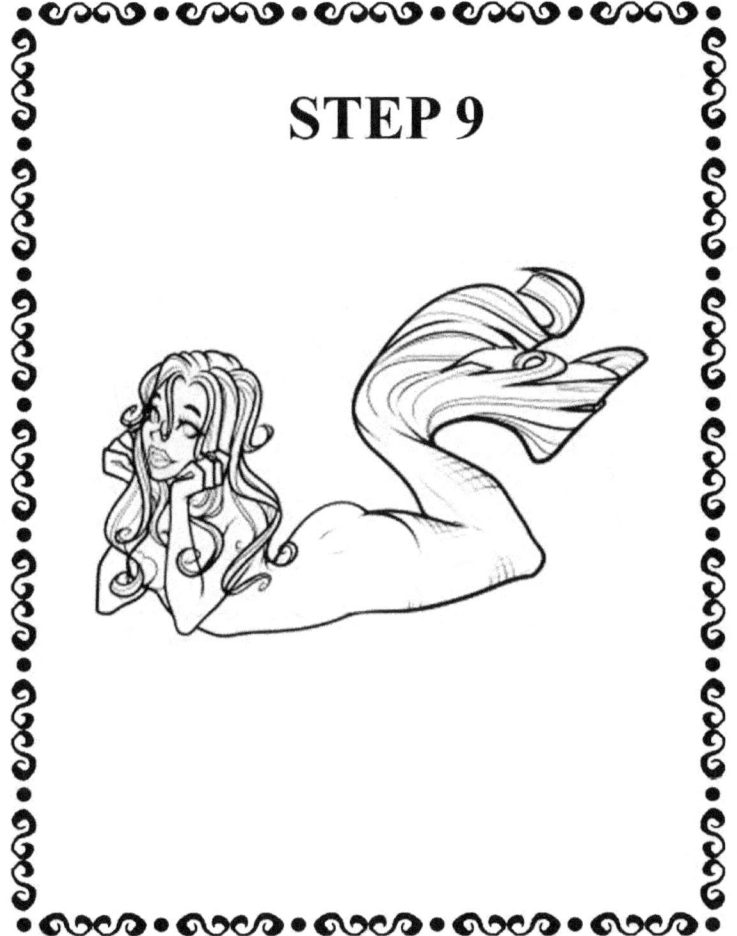

MERMAID GIRL

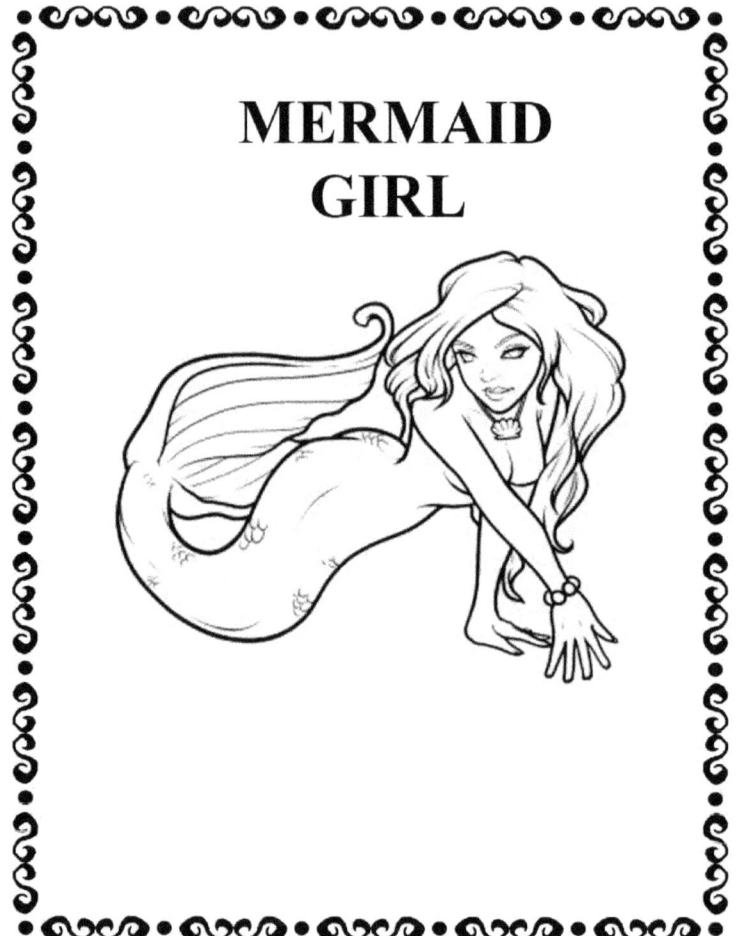

STEP 1

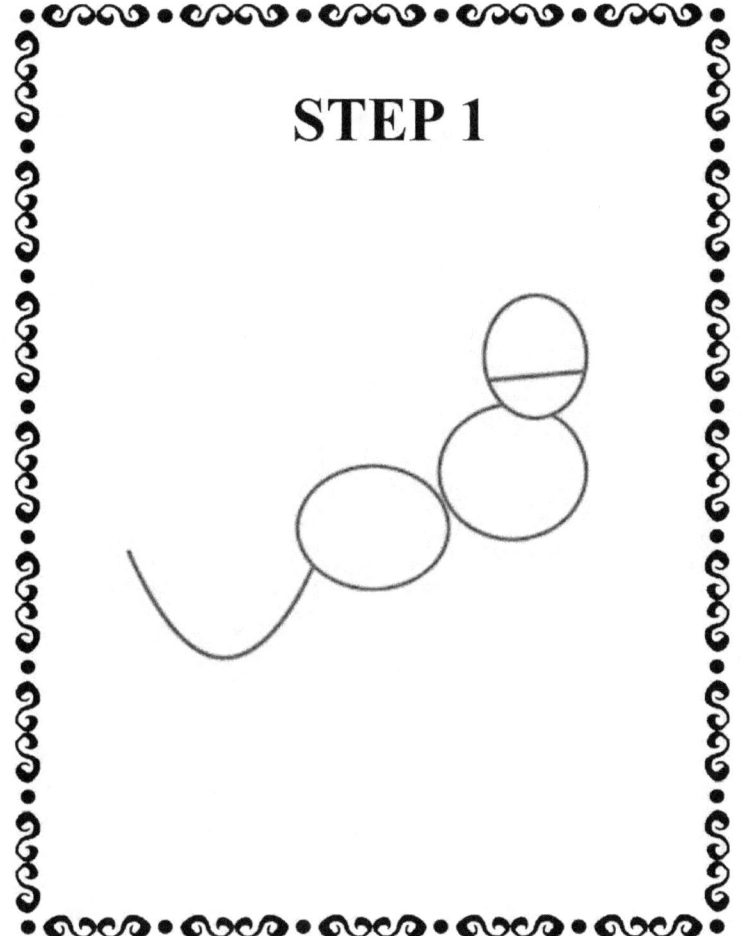

STEP 2

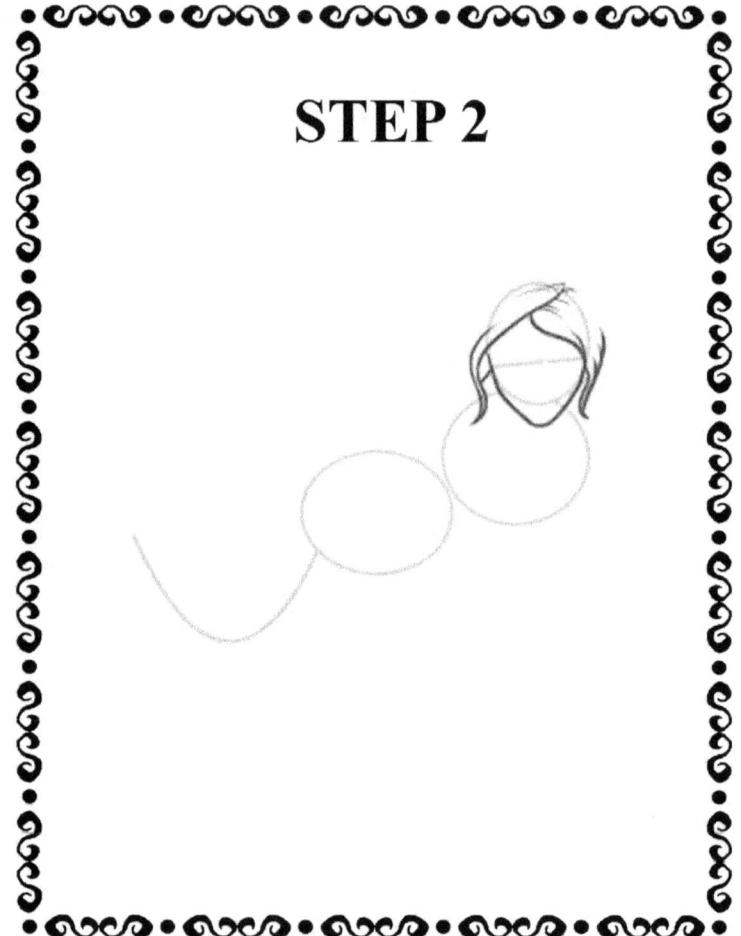

STEP 3

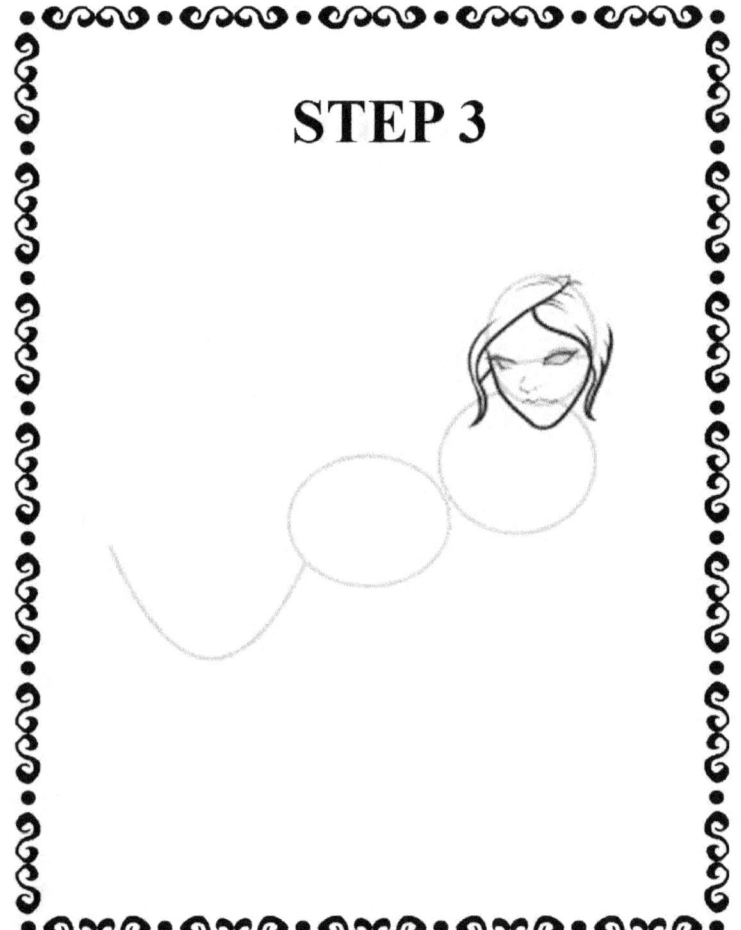

STEP 4

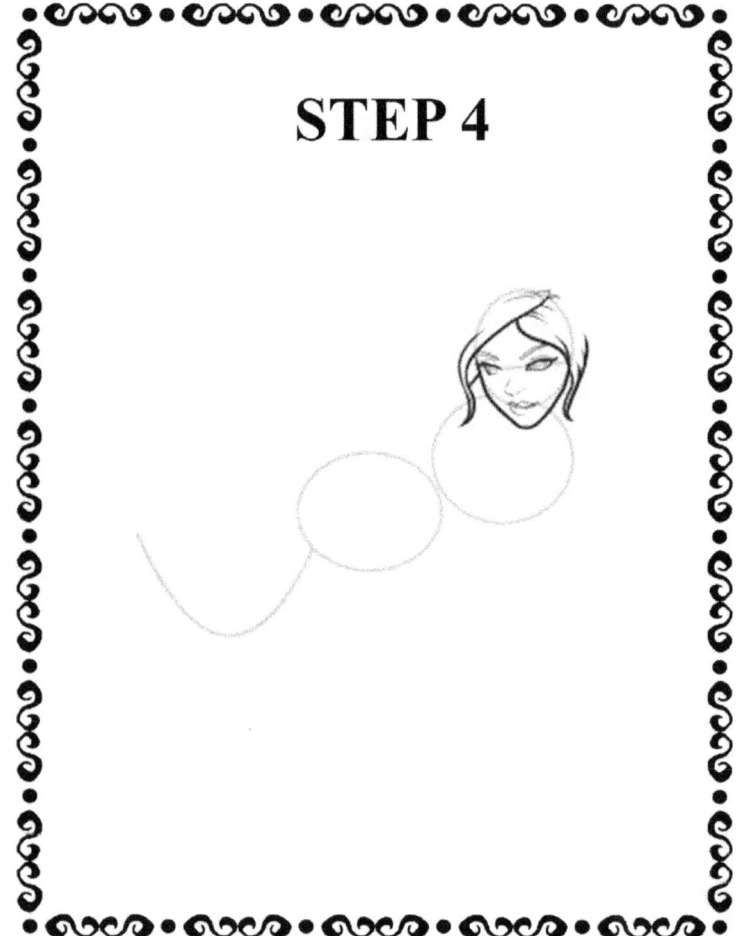

STEP 5

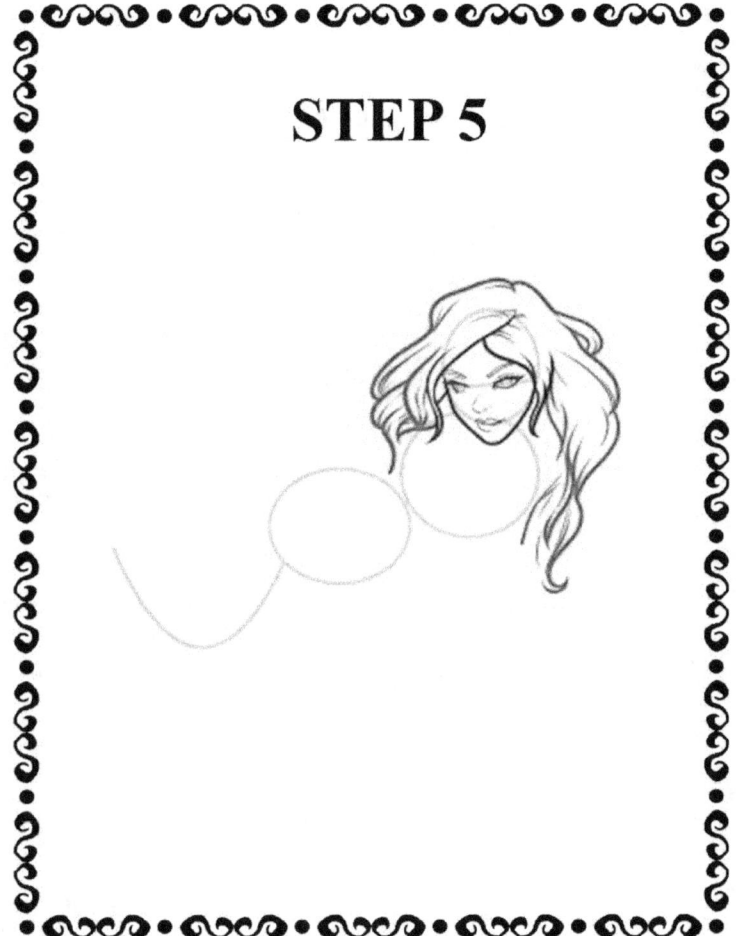

STEP 6

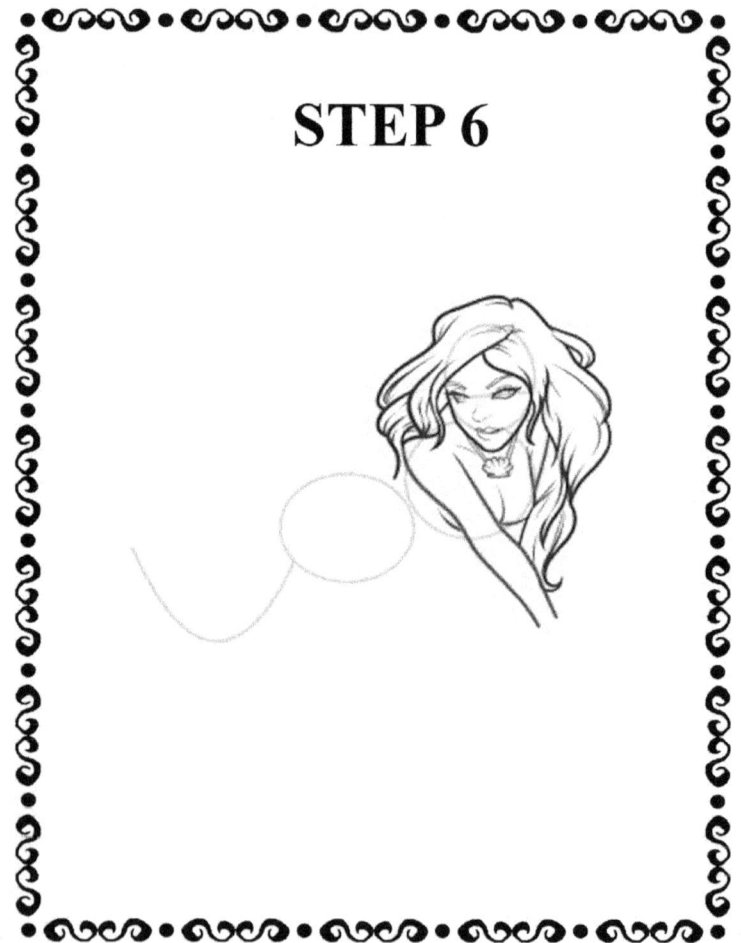

STEP 7

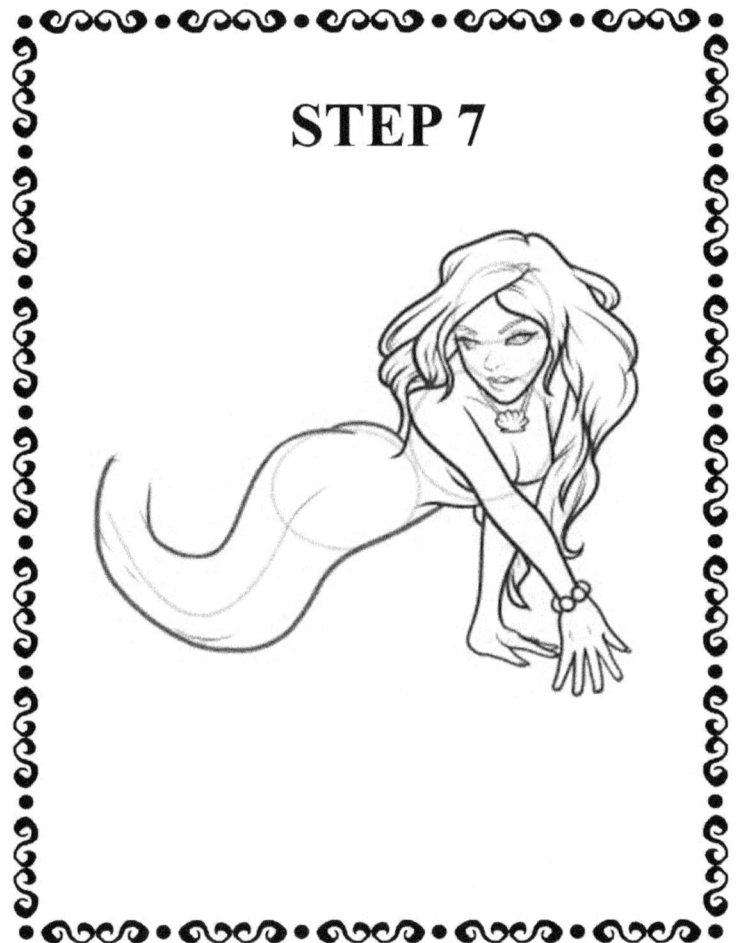

STEP 8

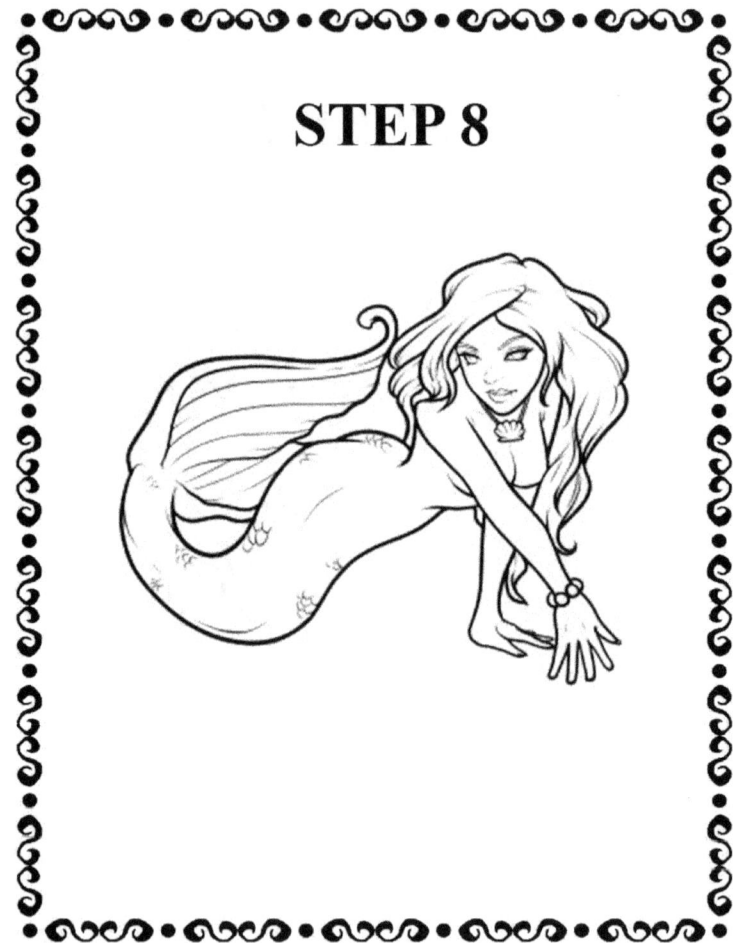

SIMPLE MERMAID

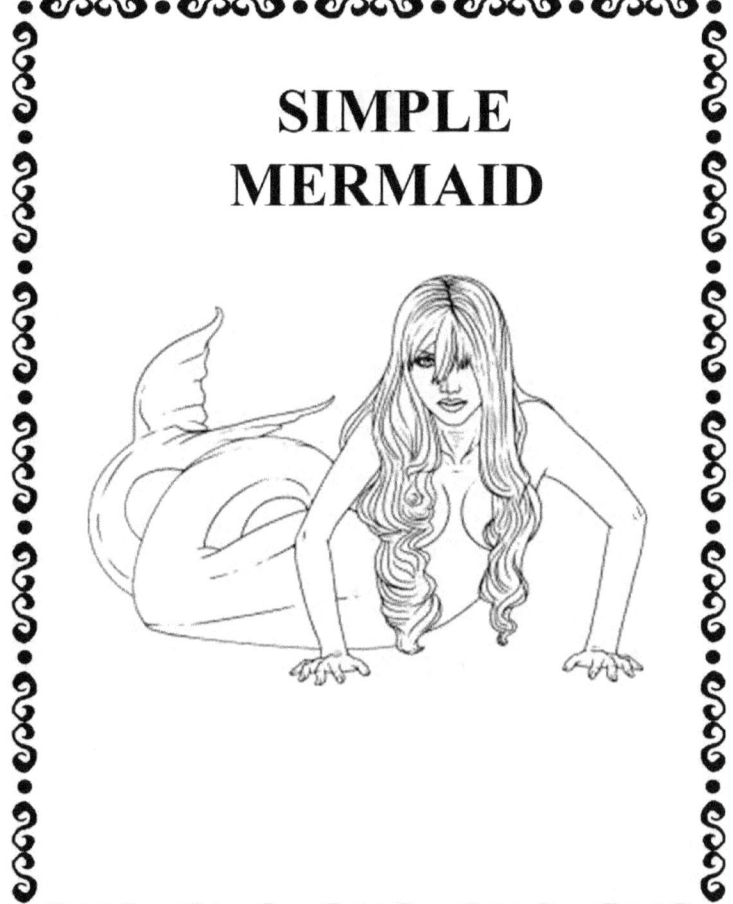

STEP 1

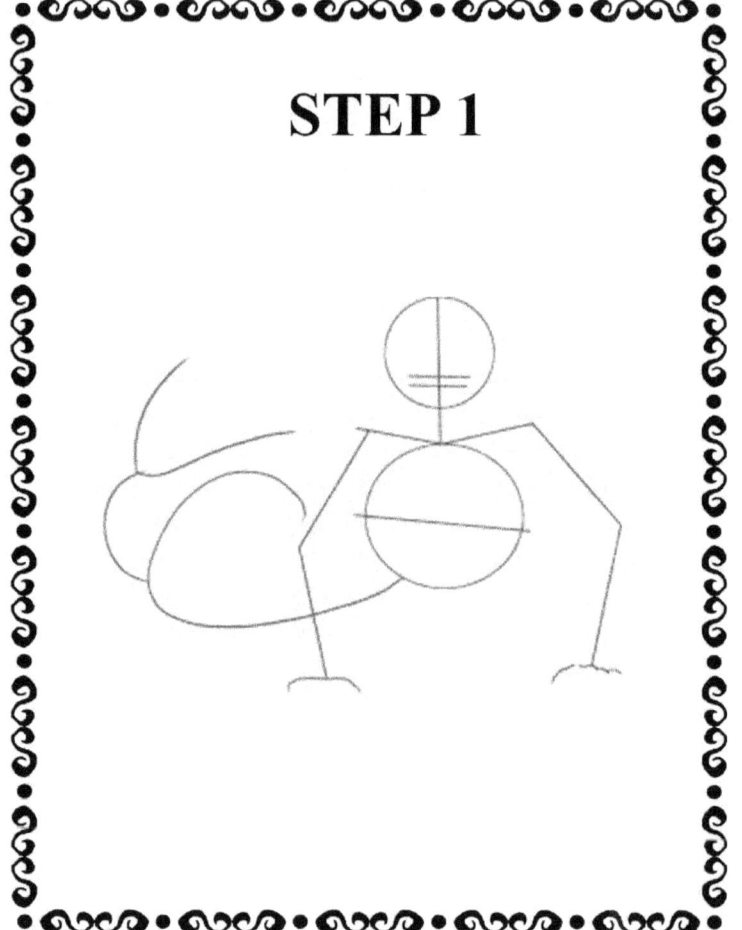

STEP 2

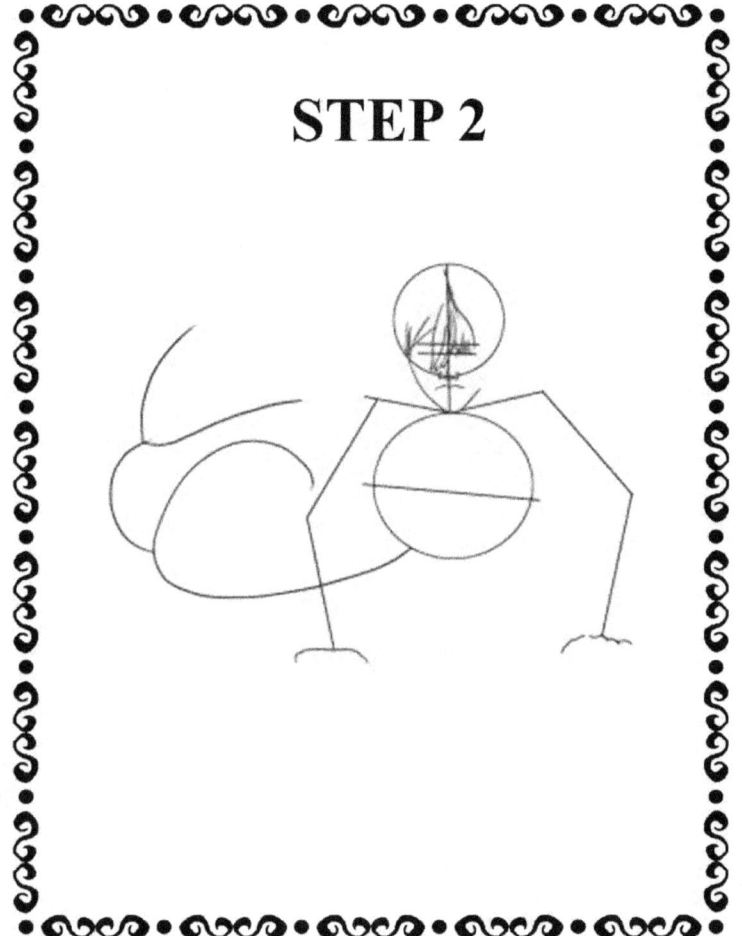

STEP 3

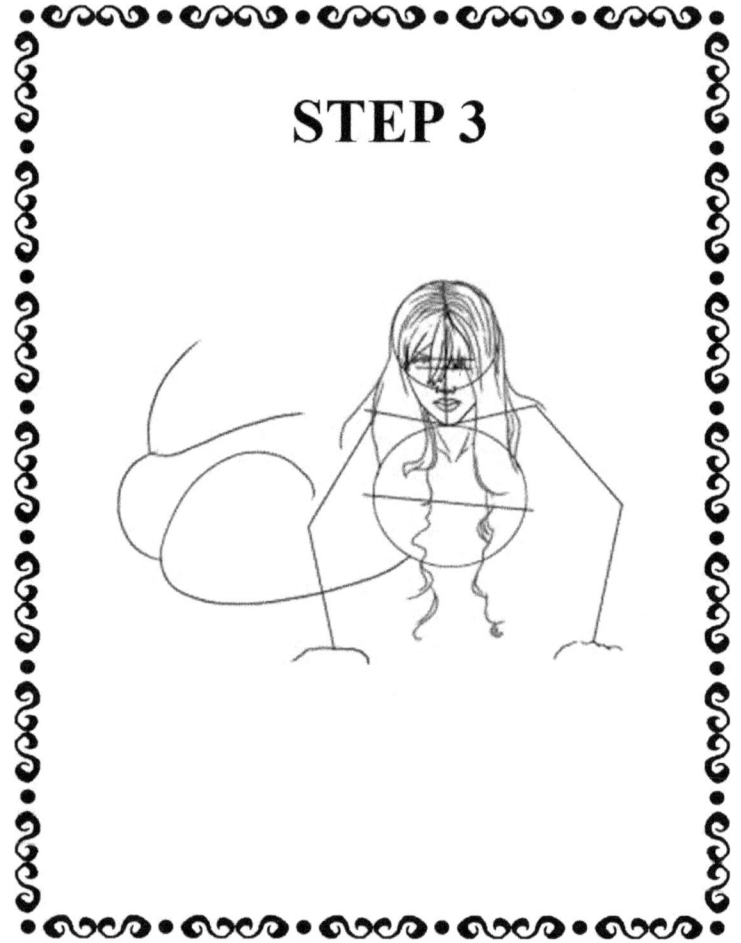

STEP 4

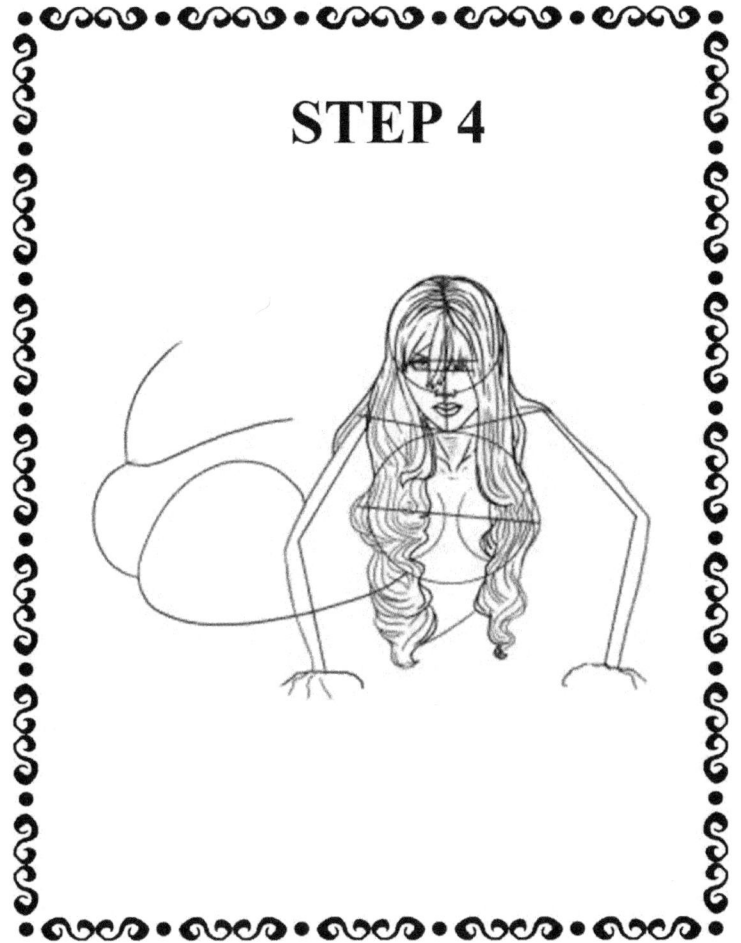

STEP 5

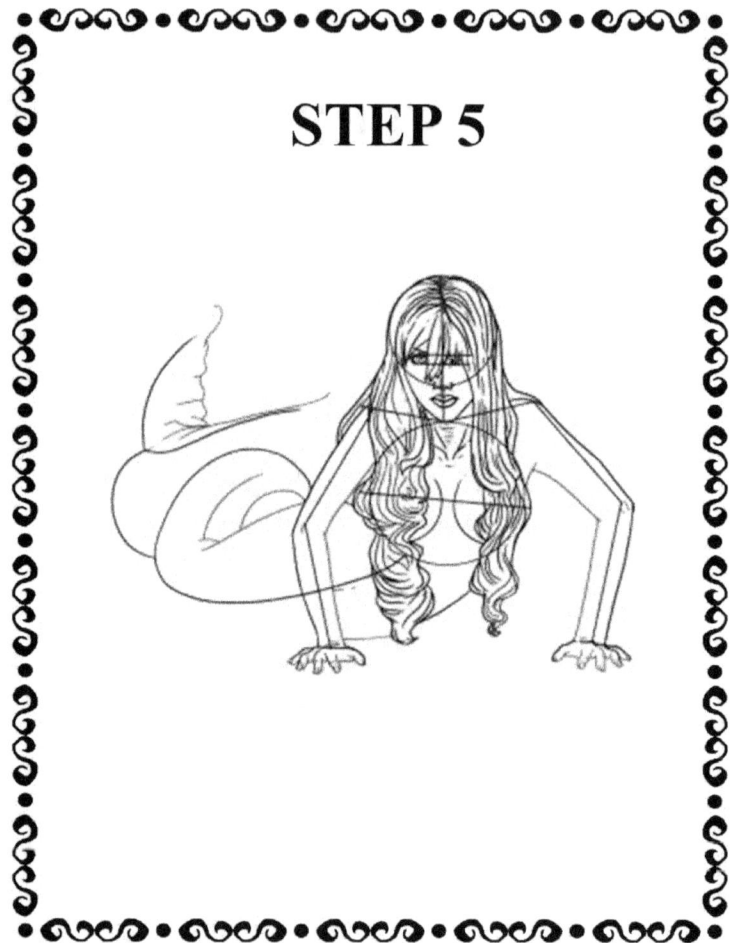

49

STEP 6

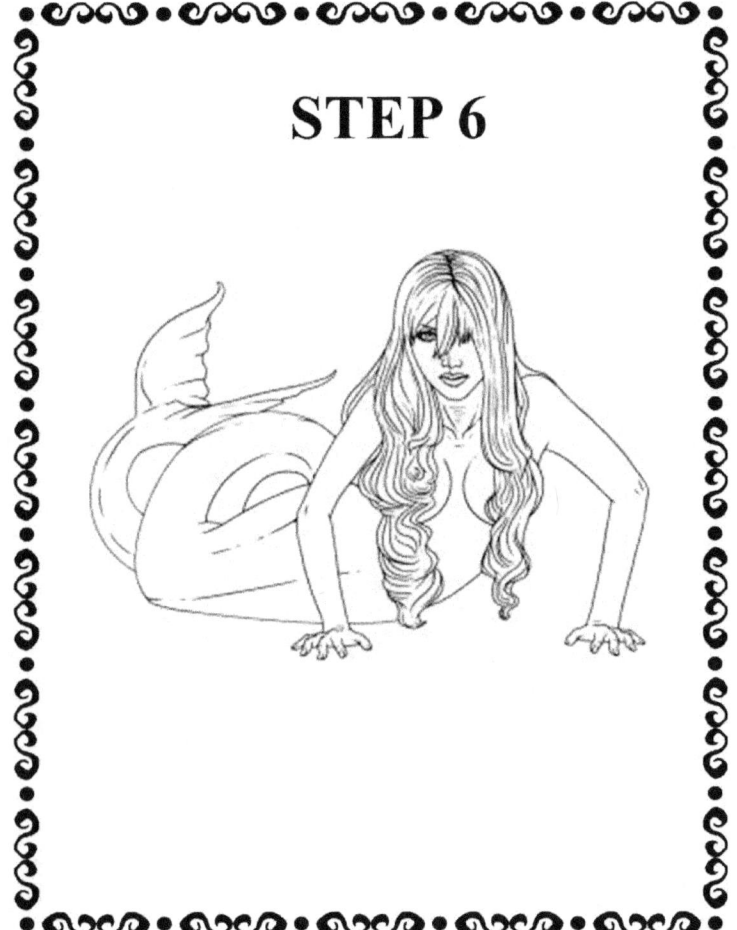

www.ingramcontent.com/pod-product-compliance
Lightning Source LLC
Chambersburg PA
CBHW071649170526
45166CB00003B/1498